Question Time

Rain Forest

Angela Wilkes

KINGFISHER
NEW YORK

Editor: Jennie Morris
Designer: Catherine Goldsmith
DTP manager: Nicky Studdart
Consultants: Chris Pellant, Norah Granger
Indexer: Jason Hook
Production Controller: Jo Blackmore
Illustrators: Lisa Alderson 8–9; Chris Forsey 4–5, 15*tl*, 28–29; Ray Grinaway 6–7, 16–17, 22–23; David Holmes 20*tl*; Stephen Holmes 17*tr*; Ian Jackson 24–25; Adam Marshall 24*tl*; Joannah May 14–15, 18–19; Terence Lambert 21*tr*; Simon Mendez 10–11; Nicki Palin 12–13; Clive Pritchard 18*bl*; Bernard Robinson 20*bl*; Eric Robson 26–27; David Wood 4*bl*.
Cartoons: Ian Dicks
Picture Researcher: Jane Lambert
Picture acknowledgments: 4*cl* Martin Harvey/NHPA; 7*cr* Bruce Coleman Collection; 10*cl* Jurgen & Christine Sohns/Frank Lane Picture Agency; 22*c* Gerald S. Cubitt/Bruce Coleman Collection; 24*bl* Alain Compost/Bruce Coleman Collection; 25*tr* Kevin Schafer/NHPA; 27*tr* Michael Fogden/www.osf.uk.com; 29*tr* Silvestris/Frank Lane Picture Agency.

Every effort has been made to trace the copyright holders of the photographs. The publishers apologize for any inconvenience caused.

KINGFISHER
Larousse Kingfisher Chambers Inc.
80 Maiden Lane
New York, New York 10038
www.kingfisherpub.com

First published in 2002
10 9 8 7 6 5 4 3 2 1

1TR/1201/TIMS/RNB(RNB)/128MA

LIBRARY OF CONGRESS CATALOGING-IN-PUBLICATION DATA has been applied for.

ISBN 0-7534-5438-6 (HC)
ISBN 0-7534-5442-4 (PB)

Printed in China

CONTENTS

ABOUT this book

Have you ever wondered how gibbons swing through trees? Have all your questions about the rain forest answered, and learn other fascinating facts on every information-packed page of this book. Words in **bold** are in the glossary on page 31.

Look and find

★ ★

angelfish

All through the book you will see the **Look and find** symbol. This has the name and picture of a small object that is hidden somewhere on the page. Look carefully to see if you can find it.

Now I know . . .

★ These boxes contain quick answers to all of the questions.
★ They will help you remember all about the amazing world of the rain forest.

WHAT is a rain forest?

A rain forest is a dense, steamy forest that grows in tropical countries where it is hot all the time. Millions of giant trees grow close together, draped in exotic plants and trailing **creepers**. It pours down rain almost everyday and there are no seasons, so the trees stay green all year round. More kinds of plants and animals live in rain forests than anywhere else.

Gibbon

WHY do the trees grow so tall?

Rain forest trees grow very fast in the hot, wet conditions. They race against each other to reach the sun's light, so they grow very tall. Most of them have long, thin trunks. They spread out their branches about 160 ft. (50m) from the ground to form a leafy **canopy**. But some giant trees called **emergents** grow even taller and tower above the rest of the forest.

Many of the smallest animals in the world, such as this tiny chameleon, live in rain forests.

Pygmy chameleon

Arrow poison frog

That's amazing!

Over half of the known animals and plants in the world live in tropical rain forests!

Rain forests are just like giant sponges. Some can soak up a massive 33 ft. (10m) of rain every year!

Scarlet macaw

Colorful macaws and toucans live high up in the forest canopy.

WHICH animals live in rain forests?

An extraordinary variety of animals live in rain forests. They range from biting insects, poisonous frogs, and snakes, to butterflies as big as birds, exotic parrots, and large **apes**. Animals live at different levels in the trees depending on where they find their food. Some roam the gloomy forest floor, while others move through the shady **understory** or spend their whole lives high in the sunny treetops.

Morpho butterflies

Leafcutter ants

Now I know . . .

★ A rain forest is a forest that grows in hot places where it rains a lot.
★ The trees grow very tall as they reach for sunlight.
★ A huge variety of different animals live in rain forests.

Look and find
★ millipede ★

WHY is it dark on the forest floor?

It is gloomy down on the floor of the rain forest because very little sunlight filters through the thick canopy of leaves above. It is hot and damp, and the air is still. The ground is covered in a layer of dead leaves, tangled roots, and young **seedlings**. In fact, it is crawling with millions of insects and tiny creatures.

WHAT are buttress roots?

Giant rain forest trees often have enormous raised roots like wooden wings around the base of their trunks. These are called **buttress roots** after the buttresses found attached to the outside of many European cathedrals, which support the walls.

Arrow poison frog

Army ants

Tapir

That's amazing!

Columns of up to 150,000 fierce army ants march across the forest floor, attacking small animals in their way!

Buttress roots can be as tall as a small house!

Tarantula

WHERE do jaguars prowl?

Jaguars are the largest cats in South America and live near rivers deep in the rain forest. They usually hunt at dawn or dusk when their patterned coats make it hard to spot them prowling through the trees. Jaguars are strong swimmers and catch fish, turtles, and even crocodiles. They also climb trees in search of monkeys and sleepy sloths.

Viceroy butterflies

Heliconia flower

Arrow poison frog

Jaguar

Now I know . . .

★ It is dark on the forest floor because little sunlight reaches it.

★ Buttress roots prop up tall rain forest trees.

★ Jaguars prowl near rivers in South American rain forests.

Look and find
cicada

HOW do plants climb trees?

Climbing plants cannot reach the forest canopy by themselves. So they cling onto trees with hooks or **tendrils** and wind their way up around tree trunks toward the sunlight. Giant woody plants called **lianas** loop from one treetop to another and drop long roots like ropes back down to the ground.

Eyelash viper

WHICH vine has poisonous leaves?

Liana

The passionflower **vine** has poisonous leaves. Postman caterpillars eat them and become poisonous too before turning into butterflies. The butterflies' red and black markings warn other animals that they are poisonous.

Postman butterfly

Heliconia flower

Passionflower

Arrow poison frog

That's amazing!

The giant aroid has heart-shaped leaves wide enough for a child to go to sleep on!

Strangler figs climb down trees by winding their roots around the trunks!

WHY do leaves grow so big?

In shady parts of the rain forest, some plants grow enormous leaves so they can catch more sunlight. This helps them grow. Leaves work best if they don't soak up water, so most leaves have waxy surfaces and points at the end called drip tips. This helps the rain run off them easily.

Strangler fig

Cheese plant

Common lancehead

Red-eyed treefrog

Now I know . . .

★ Climbing plants wind their way up trees using hooks or tendrils.
★ The passionflower vine has poisonous leaves.
★ Rain forest plants have big leaves to trap more sunlight.

9

WHO lives in the treetops?

Birds, monkeys, snakes, and many other animals live high in the treetops. Here the branches of the trees lace together to form a huge, leafy canopy with plenty of places to shelter and nest. It is hot and sunny, and there are fruit, seeds, and leaves to feed on all year round.

Emerald tree boa

Tamandua

WHERE do oropendolas nest?

Birds called oropendolas build nests like slender string baskets that hang from the trees. Female oropendolas weave the nests out of grass-shaped leaves. They attach them to the thin tips of branches, where they will be out of reach to enemies.

That's amazing!

The top of a rain forest tree can be as big as a soccer field!

Oropendolas build their nests near wasps' nests to scare off enemies!

10

Harpy eagle

Toucan

Spider monkeys

Sloth

Hummingbird

HOW do spider monkeys cling onto trees?

Spider monkeys use their arms, legs, and long, strong tails to cling onto trees. They coil their tails around branches to help them hang on while they pick fruit with their hands. Beneath the tip of their tail is a patch of bare skin like a palm of a human hand that helps it grip onto things more tightly.

Now I know . . .

★ Birds, monkeys, snakes, and many other animals live high in the treetops.

★ Oropendolas build nests that hang from tree branches.

★ Spider monkeys use their tails to cling onto trees.

11

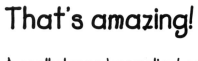
WHAT is an epiphyte?

High above the ground the branches and trunks of rain forest trees are covered in plants and flowers, like a tropical garden. These plants are called **epiphytes** or air plants. They cannot grow on the dark forest floor, but thrive high up in the treetops where there is plenty of sunlight. The epiphytes cling to the trees, using their tiny roots as anchors.

That's amazing!

A really large bromeliad can contain as much as an entire bucketful of water!

More than 28,000 different kinds of epiphytes grow on rain forest trees!

Some flowers, such as **orchids**, are epiphytes too. They often grow in the moss that lives on branches.

Orchid

HOW do epiphytes catch water?

Epiphytes have many ways of catching water. Some have spongy roots that dangle below branches and absorb water from the air. Others have giant, waxy leaves that funnel rainwater down to their roots. Spiky plants called **bromeliads** have leaves that overlap at the base to form small water tanks. Many plants trap dead leaves to make a damp layer of **compost** where they can grow.

WHERE do treefrogs hide?

During the hottest part of the day, tiny treefrogs wallow in the small puddles that collect in plants, or they hide beneath damp leaves. Puddles in bromeliads attract plenty of insects for the frogs to eat. Some puddles are deep enough for frogs to lay **frog spawn** in during the breeding season.

Now I know . . .

★ Epiphytes are plants that grow high up in the sunny treetops.
★ Epiphytes absorb water from the air or trap it in leaves.
★ Treefrogs hide in puddles in plants or under damp leaves.

WHAT do hummingbirds eat?

Hummingbirds feed on **nectar**, a sweet juice found inside flowers. Hummingbirds do not sit on flowers to feed. Instead, they hover in front of them like helicopters, beating their tiny wings up to 90 times a second. This holds them still so they can push their long beaks into the flowers and suck up the nectar.

That's amazing!

The rafflesia, the biggest flower in the world, smells like rotting meat!

Bees trapped inside bucket orchids have to follow an obstacle course to escape!

Orchid

HOW do bees help orchids?

Many bees in the rain forest feed on nectar and **pollen** from orchid flowers. As they visit flowers and gather food they carry pollen from one flower to anothe This helps the orchids make seeds, so more orchids grow

HOW do plants trap insects?

Pitcher plants trap insects and soak up the **nutrients** from them to get their food. The plants have traps shaped like pitchers or jugs that are half full of liquid. Nectar around the rims of the pitchers attracts insects. They land on the slippery rims and then fall into the liquid inside and drown.

Pitcher plant

Tiger butterfly

Bee

Now I know . . .

★ Hummingbirds feed on a juice inside flowers called nectar.

★ Bees carry pollen from one orchid flower to another.

★ Pitcher plants trap insects in their pitchers.

Look and find
★ ★
stick insect

WHICH ants collect leaves?

Trails of leafcutter ants scurry up and down the tall trees of the Amazon rain forest. These ants climb trees and bite off pieces of leaves, which they carry back down to their huge underground nests. There more ants make the leaves into a mushy compost where gardens of **fungus** grow. This fungus is food for the entire ant **colony**.

Termites

WHERE do termites live?

Millions of termites live together in colonies. Some termites build huge tree nests out of mud. Others make giant nests with tall mounds of mud above them. The mounds help air get to the nests down below.

Leafcutter ants

That's amazing!

A giant pangolin, a type of anteater, can pick up hundreds of ants at a time on its long, sticky tongue!

A colony of leafcutter ants can steal all the leaves from the top of a tree in just one day!

16

WHICH insect looks like a flower?

The flower mantis has a clever disguise—it looks just like a pink flower. The mantis hides on an orchid, pretending to be part of the flower. It keeps very still until an insect lands nearby—then it shoots out its spiny front legs to catch it. This disguise, or **camouflage**, does not only help the mantis catch food. It also makes it hard for any of its enemies to spot it.

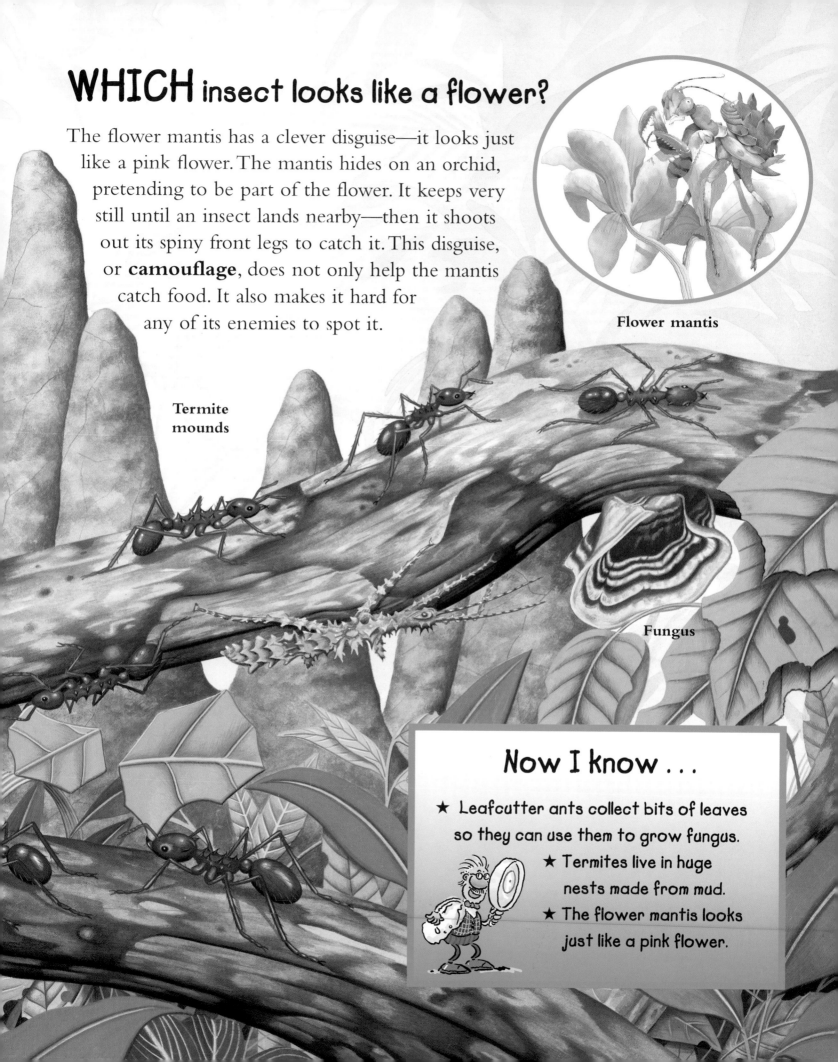

Flower mantis

Termite mounds

Fungus

Now I know . . .

★ Leafcutter ants collect bits of leaves so they can use them to grow fungus.

★ Termites live in huge nests made from mud.

★ The flower mantis looks just like a pink flower.

WHY do chameleons change color?

Chameleons are lizards that live in rain forest trees. They camouflage themselves by staying very still and changing color to match their surroundings. This makes it hard for insects to see them. Chameleons have hollow, sticky-tipped tongues as long as their bodies and tails. If an insect comes too close, their tongues shoot out and snap them up.

That's amazing!

Chameleons can swivel their eyes and look in two different directions at once!

South American Indians dip their hunting darts in poison from frogs to make them more deadly!

WHICH frogs are brightly colored?

Arrow poison frogs

Many rain forest frogs are brightly colored, but the most colorful are arrow poison frogs. These tiny frogs are highly poisonous. Their bright colors and patterns act as a warning signal to animals that might eat them, such as snakes.

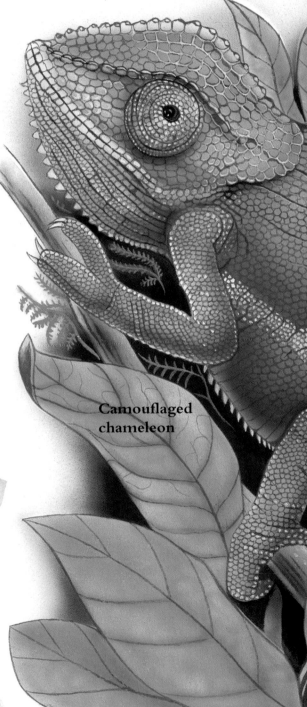

Camouflaged chameleon

Chameleon's long tongue

Reticulated python

HOW does a python hide?

The reticulated python lies without moving among the dead leaves on the forest floor. The colored patterns on its skin help it blend in with the leaves and camouflage it. The python waits for small animals, frogs, and birds to come close. It squeezes its prey to death before eating them whole.

Now I know . . .

★ Chameleons change color to help them catch food.
★ Arrow poison frogs are brightly colored.
★ The patterns on a python's skin help it hide in dead leaves.

19

WHY is a toucan's beak so big?

Toucans use their giant curved beaks to reach for juicy fruit growing on twigs too small for them to perch on. Toucans' beaks look heavy, but they are actually very light. Some people think that the dazzling rainbow colors and patterns on their beaks help them signal to each other and find a mate. Toucans like company and live in flocks.

Toco toucan

Look and find ★ ★ butterfly

WHAT do macaws and parrots eat?

Macaws and parrots eat fruits and seeds. They have powerful beaks that can crush tough nuts like a nutcracker. Parrots use their strong claws to turn nuts and seeds around while they arc eating. This makes it easier to crack them open.

Scarlet macaws

That's amazing!

Blue-crowned parrots go to sleep upside-down like bats!

Some macaws gobble poisonous fruit, then swallow special clay to stop them from getting a stomachache!

Toucans toss their heads back
to toss food down their throats.

**Keel-billed
toucan**

Male bird of paradise

WHICH birds
dance and show off?

Before birds can lay eggs they have
to find a mate. Male birds of paradise have
long, brightly-colored feathers on their wings
or tails. They compete with each other to try to
win a mate. They stand on branches and perform
dances to show females how handsome they
are. Some birds of paradise even hang upside-
down like acrobats, fanning out their
feathers and shaking them.

Toco toucan

The inside edges of a toucan's beak are
jagged so that it can grip berries firmly
or bite off chunks of large fruit.

Now I know . . .

★ A toucan uses its giant beak
to reach for fruit to eat.
★ Macaws and parrots
eat fruits and seeds.
★ Male birds of paradise show
off their feathers to win mates.

21

★ Look and find ★
thorn bugs

WHICH lizard can fly?

In some Asian rain forests animals can glide from tree to tree. Flying lizards have flaps of skin on their sides that open out like parachutes when they jump, so they can glide to lower branches. Flying snakes launch themselves into the air and flatten their bodies. Flying frogs glide by stretching out their webbed hands and feet when they jump.

WHY do slow lorises move so slowly?

Slow lorises are small, furry animals that come out to hunt at night. They creep slowly along thin branches, looking for fruit, caterpillars, and insects to eat. They move very slowly so neither insects nor enemies will spot them easily.

Slow loris

Flying snake

That's amazing!

A slow loris can freeze in one position for hours at a time to avoid being seen by an enemy!

Gibbons can turn in a complete circle just hanging from a tree with one hand!

HOW do gibbons swing through trees?

Gibbon

Gibbons are the fastest apes in the treetops. They swing through the trees by their hands, twisting their shoulders to reach the next branch. As they swing they curl up their legs. This helps them go faster. Gibbons are not very big so they can hang on to small branches and reach out for fruit growing at the tips.

When a flying lizard rests on a branch, it folds its flaps of skin back along its sides.

Flying lizard

Flying frog

Now I know . . .

★ Flying lizards in Asian rain forests can glide from one tree branch to another.

★ Slow lorises move slowly so their enemies cannot see them.

★ Gibbons swing through the trees by their hands.

Look and find ★ cockroach

WHERE do orangutans live?

Orangutans are hairy orange apes that live in the swampy rain forests of Borneo. They love juicy fruit and spend their days moving from one treetop to another looking for it. Most orangutans build two new nests a day. They make a small one for an afternoon nap, and a bigger tree den where they sleep at night.

Orangutan mother and baby

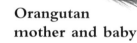

Proboscis monkey

WHICH monkey has a giant nose?

Proboscis monkeys have huge, droopy noses up to 3 in. (7cm) long. They spend hours each day sitting in mangrove trees, munching leaves. Afterward their stomachs stick out so much that they have to go to sleep until they feel better. Proboscis monkeys also love swimming. Some of them even dive into the water from the trees.

Howler monkey calling

Baby orangutans ride with their mothers until they are strong enough to climb trees by themselves. They usually stay with their mothers until they are about eight years old and fully grown.

That's amazing!

An orangutan mother often makes herself into a bridge between trees for her baby to walk across!

Howler monkeys sunbathe in the treetops to warm up at the beginning of the day!

WHY do howler monkeys make so much noise?

Howler monkeys sound like leopards roaring. They live in family groups high up in the treetops and howl to each other as the sun rises. Their calls are so loud that they can be heard almost two miles away. They howl to warn other groups of howler monkeys to keep away from their area. This could be to make sure that no other monkeys take their food.

Now I know . . .

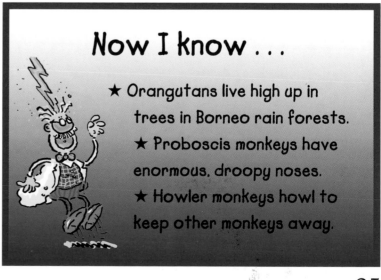

★ Orangutans live high up in trees in Borneo rain forests.
★ Proboscis monkeys have enormous, droopy noses.
★ Howler monkeys howl to keep other monkeys away.

WHICH fish have sharp teeth?

Piranhas are small fish with rows of sharp, triangular teeth. They usually eat fish, fruit, and seeds, but when there is not much food, they hunt in large groups called **shoals**. A shoal of piranhas is very dangerous. It can attack an animal and eat everything but its bones in just a few minutes.

That's amusing!

Anacondas can grow up to 33 ft. (10m) long—that's longer than a bus!

Caimans are like alligators and can float just beneath the surface of the water so other animals will think they are logs!

Capybaras

Caiman

Lungfish

Discus fish

Electric eel

26

HOW does an anaconda catch its food?

Anacondas are giant snakes that live close to rivers and swamps. They are good swimmers, but they like to lie in wait for birds and animals to come down to the water to drink. An anaconda wraps its huge body very tightly around its prey. It squeezes the animal to death before swallowing it whole.

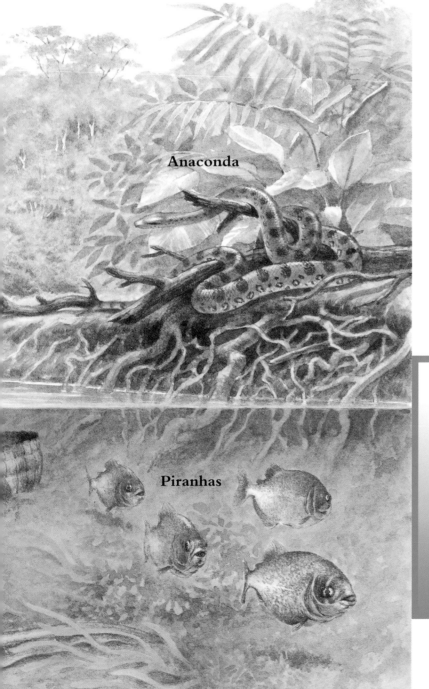

Anaconda

Piranhas

WHERE do mangroves grow?

Mangroves are strange trees that grow along the swampy banks and **estuaries** of rain forests. They thrive on the salty water, propped up on long roots like stilts that stick out sideways. Their roots anchor them firmly in the mud.

Now I know . . .

★ Piranhas are fierce fish with sharp, triangular teeth.
★ Anacondas squeeze the animals they catch to death.
★ Mangrove trees grow along the banks of rain forests.

HOW are rain forests important?

Rain forests are important for many reasons. They are home to plants and animals that live nowhere else in the world. Many everyday foods and things we use, such as coffee, cocoa, and rubber, come from rain forest plants. Other plants are used to make lifesaving medicine. The huge number of trees in rain forests also affect weather all around the world. Without rain forests, a cold area could become warmer, and a dry area could become wetter.

Golden lion tamarins

Morpho butterfly

WHICH animals and plants are endangered?

Rain forests everywhere are being cut down. When this happens, all the plants die, and many animals lose their homes and food. Some animals are also killed by hunters or captured and sold as pets. As a result, many plants and animals, from tiny insects to gorillas, are becoming very rare. Some of them, such as the golden lion tamarin, are so rare that they are in danger of dying out completely.

That's Amazing!

Every year between 15 and 20 million rain forest animals are smuggled from Brazil and sold as pets!

An area of rain forest about the size of California is destroyed around the world each year!

WHY are rain forests being destroyed?

Rain forests are destroyed so people can make money from them. Many trees are cut down because their wood is valuable. Huge areas of forests are cut down by companies mining for minerals or oil. Other areas are cleared to make farms. After a few years the land is like a desert. Nothing else will grow on it, so more trees are cut down.

Coati

Arrow poison frog

Now I know . . .

★ Rain forests contain valuable plants and animals and help control the weather.

★ Many plants and animals are becoming very rare.

★ Forests are cut down for wood, farming, and mining.

RAIN FOREST QUIZ

What do you remember about
the rain forest? Test what you know
and see how much you have learned.

1 Where do you find rain forests?
a)   in cold places
b)   in tropical countries
c)   in dry places

2 What lives on the forest floor?
a)   monkeys
b)   birds
c)   insects

3 Which plant has poisonous leaves?
a)   strangler fig
b)   cheese plant
c)   passionflower vine

4 What are epiphytes?
a)   plants
b)   insects
c)   birds

5 What do spider monkeys like to eat?
a)   fruit
b)   worms
c)   birds

6 Which plant traps insects?
a)   pitcher plant
b)   orchid
c)   passionflower vine

7 What kind of insect builds tall mounds?
a)   ant
b)   mantis
c)   termite

8 Where do chameleons live?
a)   on the ground
b)   in trees
c)   in ponds

9 Which birds have beaks like nutcrackers?
a)   birds of paradise
b)   hummingbirds
c)   macaws and parrots

10 Which ape has orange fur?
a)   chimpanzee
b)   orangutan
c)   gorilla

Find the answers on page 32

GLOSSARY

apes Animals like monkeys that do not have tails.

bromeliads Plants with overlapping, fleshy leaves like the top of a pineapple.

buttress roots Roots that form high supports around the bases of tall, rain forest trees.

camouflage A color, shape, or pattern that hides an object. A camouflaged animal looks like its surroundings, so it is hard to see.

canopy The part of a rain forest where the trees spread out their leafy branches like a roof.

colony A group of the same kinds of animal, such as ants and termites, that live together.

compost A mixture of dead leaves that is like soil.

creepers Plants that grow along the ground or climb up supports such as trees.

emergents Huge trees that grow taller than the other trees around them in the rainforest.

epiphytes Plants that grow on trees or other plants, instead of in the ground.

estuaries Areas of water where rivers meet the sea.

frog spawn Frogs' eggs protected by jelly and laid in water.

fungus A spongy plant that is not green and has no leaves or flowers. Fungi grow on other plants, especially dead ones.

lianas Climbing plants with woody stems.

nectar The sweet juice deep inside flowers that birds and insects like to eat.

nutrients The useful parts of food that all plants and animals need in order to grow and to be healthy.

orchids Exotic flowers with waxy petals that often grow on rain forest trees, like epiphytes.

pollen A sticky, yellow powder made by flowers. Pollen has to travel or be carried from one flower to another in order for seeds to grow.

seedlings Young plants that have grown from seeds.

shoals Large groups of fish that swim and eat together.

tendrils The small, threadlike parts of climbing plants that reach out to trees and wrap themselves around them.

understory The shady, lower part of a rain forest beneath the branches of the trees.

vine A tall climbing or trailing plant with long, flexible stems.

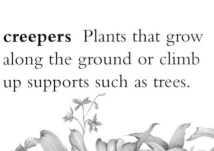

INDEX

Answers to the Rain Forest Quiz on page 30

★ 1 b ★ 2 c ★ 3 c ★ 4 a ★ 5 a ★ 6 a ★ 7 c ★ 8 b ★ 9 c ★ 10 b